121

CARRY ON

CARRY ON

Reflections for a New Generation

JOHN LEWIS

WITH KABIR SEHGAL

FOREWORD BY
AMBASSADOR ANDREW YOUNG

GRAND CENTRAL
PUBLISHING

NEW YORK   BOSTON

Grand Central Publishing
Hachette Book Group
1290 Avenue of the Americas, New York, NY 10104
grandcentralpublishing.com
twitter.com/grandcentralpub

First Edition: July 2021

Grand Central Publishing is a division of Hachette Book Group, Inc. The Grand Central Publishing name and logo is a trademark of Hachette Book Group, Inc.

Interior illustrations by Sarah Congdon
Print book interior design by Thomas Louie

The publisher is not responsible for websites (or their content) that are not owned by the publisher.

The Hachette Speakers Bureau provides a wide range of authors for speaking events. To find out more, go to www.hachettespeakersbureau.com or call (866) 376-6591.

Library of Congress Cataloging-in-Publication Data has been applied for.

ISBNs: 978-1-5387-0712-8 (hardcover), 978-1-5387-0714-2 (ebook)

Printed in the United States of America

LSC-C

Printing 1, 2021

CONTENTS

CONTENTS

FOREWORD

by Ambassador Andrew Young

One of the reasons I came back to the South from New York, where I was working for the National Council of Churches, was the Nashville sit-in, in 1960. And there was John Lewis, leading it. He was persuasive and powerful even back then. There was a certain power in his humility that you were not prepared for. He just had such a sweet spirit. It was magnetic.

I remember in 1960 being on the Fisk University campus, and there was this one group of about ten students led by John Lewis, and they were preparing to leave the campus. I asked a fellow student, "Where are they going?" And he responded, "That's John Lewis, and he's going to test one of the last restaurants that we have not been able to desegregate."

It was like he ignored everything about college life and focused on desegregation. And then he got elected president of the SNCC (Student Nonviolent Coordinating Committee), in 1963. There were all of these other firebrand types who were competing for leadership, and nobody could agree on any of them. But they could all agree on John Lewis.

I watched him grow through the years since then, and he never changed.

I knew John for sixty years, and we were always close, but we didn't always agree on everything. He was very stubborn and determined. For example, when I was the mayor of Atlanta and John was on the city council, I was trying to build about four hundred new roads, including the Presidential Parkway and Freedom Parkway. They seemed like necessities for a growing metropolis. And I was catching hell all over the city trying to put together the votes in favor of these roads, and I could never get John's vote because he had made a promise to his constituents that he would not vote for more roads. He always kept his word. He was unwavering in his determination once he set his course. Now, I thought he was wrong on that, and I still do. So, to get even, we named the Freedom Parkway for him. And we're trying to name one of the buildings at Georgia State for him, because if there's one thing that's missing in American education, it's that there's no concept of humility. John Lewis embodied humility.

In fact, *HUMILITY* should be the title of this book.

You should know about John's simple determination and single-mindedness. There's a book we read in seminary by Kierkegaard. The title of it is *Purity of Heart Is to Will One Thing*. And that's the way John dealt with any issue: He focused on whatever was absolutely spiritually essential. And he didn't care what was popular, and he didn't care what was political. He didn't even care what the majority might have thought right, because the majority of Black students and leaders in Nashville did not agree with the sit-ins when they started. That didn't deter John.

And in the 1965 march from Selma to Montgomery, the SNCC voted not to participate. They were playing movement politics and ego politics. That didn't deter John.

He said, "Well, I'm not marching as the chairman of SNCC. I'm marching as John Lewis. I'm a citizen of Alabama, and I'm going to make that march." He ended up leading it with Hosea Williams, another prominent civil rights activist.

When John was not yet eighteen, he sent a letter to Dr. Martin Luther King Jr., who answered him and sent him money for a bus ticket to come to Montgomery to visit his church. And Martin took him home to dinner after the church service.

That's how impressive a kid he was. And that's how Martin and John met. Two giants of the civil rights movement.

I never knew John to show anger or frustration. He had the kind of purity of heart that Kierkegaard described. And he had it since he was that teenager.

Throughout his life, he remained the same innocent, dedicated, visionary child who went to see Martin Luther King Jr. He was the same way in Congress. He could go to anybody's congressional district and draw a crowd. Everybody wanted to meet him because everyone wants to meet one good man.

And John Lewis was one good man.

The basis of his power in Congress was that he was able to get anybody reelected. He would take his weekend and go campaign with Democrats, and probably would for Republicans, too, if they were people he believed in.

He was one of the people in Congress whom

everybody agreed with, because he was as close to a saint as they'd ever seen in Washington. He was more like the Dalai Lama or Gandhi than a politician.

And when he wasn't helping people, he was reading the Bible, because he'd always wanted to be a preacher. And in many ways he was a preacher. It was spiritual with John. It was a magnetic spirituality that drew people to him. You would rarely hear him laugh out loud. His laugh was very guarded, but he always had a twinkle in his eye, and he always seemed to be very happy. He wasn't in any way argumentative or aggressive. It was almost like he thrived on lacking an aggressive personality.

And yet, he wasn't at all righteous. He didn't expect you to be like him. He just had a sense of duty, responsibility, and discipline.

In my generation—the generation of John and Martin Luther King Jr.—we were taught that to lead a movement, there was no compromising on any principle. That it is important to forgive because you can't receive forgiveness yourself if you can't forgive others. But we had to work pretty hard to forgive the people who murdered Martin Luther King Jr.

We never lost hope. John never did. One of the musts in the movement was that whenever someone is killed, you have to continue his work. Otherwise you're sending a message that killing will stop the movement. Whenever somebody's killed, you've got to replace him with eight or ten or twenty others, or a hundred of us. So we were duty bound to have another march in Memphis, and to go on to Washington with the Poor People's Campaign in 1968, even knowing that it would not succeed. We were going there knowing we would get tear-gassed out of there and worse. John knew. You've seen those images of John. Like you see the images today. John would say to you: "Don't give up. Don't lose hope. Be patient and persevere. Change will come." Just read the following pages of wisdom by John—in his own words. These pages embody the John I knew from the beginning. He remained true to himself. Pure. Simple. Real. Humble.

John was just a rare bird down to the smallest detail. I think even in the days of the movement, when he was leading that march, everybody else might have been in blue jeans—we were about to be tear-gassed—but John was in a suit.

As I write this, COVID and social injustice have certainly humbled the most powerful nation on the face of the earth. No other nation could defeat us in war or in business or in peacemaking or anything else. But these two plagues have brought us all to our knees. Falling back on Scripture: "Be still, and know that I am God" (Psalm 46:10). We forgot who the Lord of the universe is, that this is our Father's world and it doesn't belong to us.

We're going to have to change the way we face life and think about it. I hope you find your generation's John Lewis. This is a time when we need one because there's a lot to do.

I know that right up until the end, John remained dedicated to that effort—it was in his blood and soul. He was saving his energy to try to make votes in Congress for the 2020 elections. He was determined to keep his eyes on the prize for all of you—and he wouldn't allow himself to be distracted until the good work was done. And "good trouble, necessary trouble," as John called it, had been made.

August 2020

EDITOR'S NOTE

by Gretchen Young

Some years ago I had the pleasure of hearing Congressman John Lewis speak at two separate events, and both times I was awestruck. The words he spoke, his intonations, his silences and crescendos, and his facial expressions all combined to create a unique and deeply moving oratorical experience. Soon after, I reached out to Congressman Lewis to discuss a potential book about his philosophy of nonviolence. Despite the demands of an overloaded schedule, he liked the idea, and the result was *Across That Bridge: Life Lessons and a Vision for Change*, which proved to be one of the most rewarding projects of my editorial career.

In early 2020, Congressman Lewis agreed to do another book. By then he knew he had little time left, but he decided that preserving his final thoughts on what mattered most to him would help his message to live on. So, while pushing through bouts of exhaustion, he carved out precious time for this project, and *Carry On: Reflections for a New Generation* was born.

During our interviews for this book, he spoke on a wide range of topics, from love and friendship, to justice and courage, to his favorite books and art. He reflected on the civil rights movement, the Black Lives Matter protests, and the need for equality. He also spoke of those personal qualities and characteristics needed to give back and to make positive change. He offered new messages and inspirations, and he also recounted a number of familiar stories because he enjoyed sharing them—they were his favorites, and, as such, they say the most about his legacy as he perceived it.

I will be forever grateful for the irreplaceable time he so generously set aside for this book. Like everyone else who appreciated John Lewis, I was heartbroken when he passed, in July of 2020. It felt shockingly sudden, despite my knowing how ill he was, because it was so hard to imagine our world without his magnificent, unrelenting example to light the way forward.

We all wanted to be able to lean on his strength forever, of course, but as a poet friend of mine observed, "He gave us more than enough. We just have to live up to the lessons."

ON GOOD DAYS

A good day is waking up!

It's awakening to the world and realizing the possibility that every day brings. You can write your own script and determine how you live each moment. And how you will respond to the people and events throughout your day. You don't have to jump ahead and think always about the future. Take in and absorb every moment, and you'll find yourself noticing little things—whether it's the birds chirping, the dew on the grass, the sweetness of morning, or the wind blowing on your face and skin.

I have a daily routine. While working in Congress, I get up around five o'clock in the morning in my house in Washington, DC. Every morning I read five newspapers. I walk a few blocks to the Capitol and do my workout in the gymnasium, walking on the treadmill and lifting weights. I get to my office around eight o'clock and we have a staff meeting. The days are filled with meetings and hearings. I meet with constituents, activists, other members, and policy makers. Sometimes I have a few lunch meetings per day. I sit on committees and we listen to testimony and we ask questions of the witnesses. In the evening, I am scheduled for interviews with journalists. I attend receptions and fund-raisers for various causes.

On the weekends, I have tried to get back to my district in Atlanta to meet with the people whom I represent and who sent me to Congress. And I spend time with my son.

More recently, I am undergoing treatment for my cancer diagnosis and meeting with doctors and medical staff. But I always prioritize my work as a congressman and doing the work of and for the people.

Some days are better than others, and while that is always true of any life, for me, right now, it is ever more so. Indeed, waking up is a good day. Being alive.

ON MENTORS

D r. Martin Luther King Jr. was my mentor. He, more than anyone else, helped make me the person who I am today.

Dr. King taught us that we must have love in our hearts and for our fellow brothers and sisters. He taught us all so much about how to live through his actions and words. He freed and liberated Blacks and whites and everyone from a culture of division into one of unity.

If I could say something to Dr. King today, I would say, "Hello, Dr. King, how are you?" And then I would say, "Thank you. Thank you for all that you did for us to improve our country and our world, for leading by example and showing us how to live with freedom and compassion, and how to die with conviction and grace." I would catch him up on this year 2020 especially and say, "Look at the progress we've made and look at the

work we still have to do. We've been remember-
ing your example and listening to your words. We
can still hear you. I hear you every day."

Young people today can look to people in their
families and in their communities to find mentors.
You don't have to have all the answers. You don't
have to know everything. You already know in
your heart what is right and good, what is decent,
just, fair. If you want to grow, find someone who
has walked the walk. A mentor is a sounding
board who gives you direction and guidance, and
who asks you questions for you to work out on
your own. We all need mentors. We stand on the
shoulders of those who came before us.

The time will come when you will need to
become a mentor to the next generation. Pass on
what you've learned to those who are assuming
the mantle. Pass the torch, because the fight never
ends. I make every effort to write, teach, and
advise those who are involved in the Black Lives
Matter movement so that they can learn about

how we acted according to the dictates of our heart in the 1960s during the civil rights movement. We can all learn how to be nonviolent and take the high road. That takes work, training, guidance, and mentorship.

It's always a good time to be with someone: Listen to someone without interrupting them, and then show them the way to respond to what's in their hearts. We must all develop the next generation because they are the stewards of the house of humanity, the global house. They will determine the course of freedom and justice for all.

Find a mentor. Be a mentor.

On Heroes

Mahatma Mohandas Gandhi is one of my heroes. He had great teachers, and he was also a great teacher himself. He taught us the way of peace, the way of love. He changed the course of his country and history by his rugged determination, by adhering to a spiritual practice based on finding the truth. In order to find that truth, he did away with many of the trappings of material life, gave up his career as a lawyer, and embarked upon a journey of "knowing thyself." Gandhi had soul force. He was able to take on the powers that be, knowing that his soul was connected to the divine. He knew that right was on his side.

Gandhi taught the world about the philosophy and discipline of nonviolence. This is a powerful philosophy that influenced Dr. King and those of us in the movement. Gandhi relied on non-violence to expose the world to the colonial subjugation that his country faced. And in turn, he helped to make the world a much better, more peaceful place for all of mankind. Gandhi was our hero in the movement because he found his truth and lived by his values. When Dr. King traveled to India in 1959, he said: "To other countries I may go as a tourist, but to India I come as a pilgrim." I watched a movie about Gandhi where he marched to the sea, and that reminded me of our march from Selma. His presence was always with us.

People ask if they can touch me to see if I am human, and I respond by saying, "Very much so." When I go to the grocery store with my son, he tells me to put on a hat so that people won't recognize me. But that never works, either. My son says that he doesn't want to go shopping with me because of the time it takes to shake everyone's hands, hug them, and kiss them. I don't consider what I did during the civil rights protests to be heroic—it was necessary. But it's a positive thing if my actions inspire others to be heroic.

ON GOOD TROUBLE

Growing up in Troy, Alabama, I would see signs that said "whites" and "colored." I'd ask my parents and grandparents about these signs, and they would tell me that's just the way it is. They told me, "Don't get in trouble. Don't upset the order of things."

But then I heard about Rosa Parks. She got into "good trouble." She wouldn't move to the back of the bus, which led to the Montgomery Bus Boycott. She launched the movement in earnest by doing what she knew in her heart was right. I met Rosa Parks in 1957, when I was just seventeen. I met Dr. Martin Luther King Jr. the following year, after I wrote him a letter.

And I've been getting into good trouble ever since. I have been arrested over forty times— forty-five if you include the arrests while in Congress. Those first arrests made me feel so liberated and free. In 1961 I was in Nashville, and I was arrested for sitting at the counter of a Woolworth's diner. In those days, Blacks were not allowed to sit at the counter, and I was pushed, mocked, and bullied by those who opposed my actions. By the end of the day, there were almost one hundred of us who were arrested. I knew that what I was doing was morally right, and that it was only a matter of time until this truth was more widely recognized and accepted.

I have been kicked and beaten. But I never grew angry. I sought good trouble not as a form of revenge or retribution or to settle any score.

Good trouble is about dramatizing something that needs changing and correcting. My arrests help to raise awareness for the wrongs happening around the world. In 2006, four decades after my first arrests, I was arrested by the Secret Service with other members of the Congressional Black Caucus for demonstrating for an end to the conflict in Darfur, Sudan. An injustice anywhere is an injustice to all of us.

I've also helped to bring good trouble into the halls of Congress. Americans are tired of the gun violence that has gripped the nation, which has led to too much pain and suffering, too many deaths of young people. In the summer of 2016, we in Congress organized a sit-in on the floor of the House of Representatives, with 170 members joining. We used nonviolence to fight to end gun violence. Too many innocent young souls have been slain by guns and the resulting inaction on this issue.

While we didn't get a vote on measures and bills that would help to stem gun violence, our fight is not over, and we did some good. We helped to inspire and educate millions of people around the country, and we showed them that we take this issue seriously and that there are elected representatives who want to do something about it. We have to keep our eyes on the prize and return more determined than before. We will keep going and going, getting into good trouble until more join our cause and change is finally at hand. For example, after decades of efforts and protests, Mississippi finally took the Confederate emblem off their state flag, and now there is a national conversation about removing symbols of division from our cities and military bases. This is progress.

What is something that needs fixing in our country? What doesn't sit right in your hearts that moves you to protest in a nonviolent way? What can you do to get into good trouble? There is a light inside of you that will turn on when you get into good trouble. You will feel emboldened and freed. You will realize that unjust laws cannot stop you. These laws cannot stop the truth that is in your heart and soul.

ON ACTIVISM

Y ou have the right to protest for what is right. You know what I say: When you see something that is not right, not fair, not just, you have to say something, you have to do something. You have to push, and pull, and be prepared to make a little noise. When you see something that is not the way it should be, don't be afraid. Speak up, speak out, be courageous. It's a total commitment. No compromise. Just go for it.

I know something about marching. Some decades ago, when I was younger and had more hair, I marched. I marched to protest what I knew in my heart was wrong. I marched in Selma. I marched in Washington, DC. I have marched all over the country. And I've never stopped marching. Never stop marching.

The call of history is sounding again. It was sad and painful for me to watch the killing of George

Floyd. It made me cry, as he lay on the ground, with life leaving his body. How many more? How many more young Black men and women will be murdered? This madness must stop.

Black Lives Matter protesters are sending a very strong message to the world that we will stand up against injustice again and again. We will keep marching until we get to a place of peace and equality. Young Black Americans can find hope in the actions of young people across our country and the world. They are speaking up, speaking out, and getting involved. The young people who are marching, protesting, and demonstrating their activism will be an inspiration to future generations. The activists are setting an example and writing the history of our country. This gives me hope. We did it before and we will keep doing it.

People all around the world are marching in solidarity. That's because they know we live in one house, the world house. If there is an injustice to someone here, it's an injustice to us all. People will never forget what happened to George Floyd and the too many other victims. More and more folks are understanding what the struggle is all about.

During the 1960s, we protested with non-violent methods. There is something peaceful, cleansing, and wholesome about being orderly and not threatening. It means standing up with a sense of self-worth and dignity. Yes, we were jailed, arrested, firebombed, bloodied. But we never felt hate, and even though it can be hard to hold back our anger, it is worth the effort because it works in the end. We changed America, and now the time has come for more change.

Marchers today are Black, white, Latino Americans, Asian Americans, and Native Americans, and they have every orientation and come from every socioeconomic status. They are all marching to redeem the soul of the nation, to create a society at peace with ourselves. Today's marchers are drawing attention to the reality that we must make the world a safer, more peaceful place. We've come this far. And we're not going back. The world is watching. We're moving forward. Sometimes it happens slowly, steadily, but surely, and you don't even see it, and other times it happens like a loud thunderstorm. We're in a thunderstorm now, but we will make it right.

We have to be bold. We have to ask questions of the powers that be. What interests are you trying to protect? Are you on the right side of history? When we hear an unjust answer or a deafening silence, we will take to the streets and protest until change comes.

As I've said before to all the rioters throughout the nation, I understand your anger and dismay. It is a brutal reality that young, unarmed Black people are victims of institutionalized violence. It is a travesty and a tragedy.

Destruction doesn't work. Rioting isn't a movement. We must be constructive and not destructive. Chaos is sowing more division and discord.

At the 1963 March on Washington, I had a line in my prepared remarks that we would march on the South like Sherman did [General William Sherman, who burned the city of Atlanta during the Civil War], but we would do it in a non-violent way. The archbishop of the Diocese of Washington, DC, said he wouldn't give the invocation if that line remained in my speech. Dr. King and A. Philip Randolph [a prominent civil and labor rights activist] asked me to remove the line. Dr. King said that the line didn't sound like me. I couldn't say no to them, and they gave me good, sound advice. I listened. Always listen. I believed in nonviolence, and I didn't need to use that imagery.

When you burn down a building or topple a car, the violence drowns out the injustice of what's being done to you. It puts you on the same moral level as the people whose violence you are protesting. You're no longer on the higher ground or plane. You make enemies of the people you need to win over to effect change.

I've said to get organized, make a plan. Sit in, stand up. Be fierce. Be stubborn. Get out the vote. Our work is never easy. It's hard. When you move in the direction of the good, more will come to the cause. It may not happen overnight, or in a few days, weeks, or years. But have faith that your good work will be a drop in the river that will eventually break the dam, ushering in a more peaceful world.

ON JUSTICE

For far too long, Black people and other people of color have repeatedly been denied equal justice under the law. We cannot sit idly in the face of violence and injustice.

My home state of Georgia and the nation are grieving the deaths of Ahmaud Arbery, Rayshard Brooks, Breonna Taylor, George Floyd, Sandra Bland, Trayvon Martin, Tamir Rice, Philando Castile, Jordan Davis, and many more. We should say all their names and repeat them. We have pain and anguish. This burden is heavy and all consuming. It cannot be.

I have never stopped thinking about Emmett Till, a fourteen-year-old boy who endured false accusations, a sham trial, and death by lynching in 1955. And here we are over sixty years later, and young, unarmed Black men are again being falsely accused and killed by the very people who are supposed to protect them.

The country is awakening to the brutal truth. Young people are taking to the streets and assuming the mantle that is all too familiar to those of us who marched half a century ago. We cannot ignore them. We cannot let their cries for justice fall on deaf ears. They are marching for justice, for freedom, and for equality under the law.

We must practice what we preach. If we believe in life and liberty, then we should not defer the dream of equality and justice under the law for people of color. We must use the system of government to improve our laws and make our society fairer and more just. While no one bill can right the many wrongs, we can stitch together partial solutions to deal with the complex societal issues that lead to systemic bias and inequality.

We must work with law enforcement so the police become guardians—not warriors—in our communities. They need not be deputized and militarized. Instead, we need there to be more compassion, empathy, and understanding in our justice system.

We need to work with prosecutors, examine sentencing guidelines, and embark upon meaningful criminal justice reform. Judges should have more leeway when sentencing nonviolent offenders. Too often people plead guilty even when they are innocent so they can escape the complexities of the system. We have to provide inmates opportunities to redeem and rehabilitate themselves.

There is much work ahead. But our mandate is clear. We cannot thrive as a democracy when justice is reserved for only those with means. If we don't respond to these calls for justice, we will fail the people whom we represent.

ON COURAGE

Courage reflects your spirit. It reflects something deep within all of us who would rather defy an authority than go along with something that is morally wrong. Raw courage makes us stand up and speak out in the face of fear. Courage helps us overcome doubts and reservations. It's not something that comes from reason or logic but is borne from the heart and the divine purpose to take the right path.

As a child, I remember hearing the Scripture: "Sorrow may endure for a night, but joy cometh in the morning" [Psalm 30:5]. I whispered this to myself during the most harrowing moments of the movement. In May 1961, we Freedom Riders were locked in the First Baptist Church in Montgomery, Alabama, because there was an angry mob of men waiting outside the church who were brandishing baseball bats and lead pipes. We thought that we were going to die right there.

But that morning President John F. Kennedy saved us when he federalized the Alabama National Guard. Federal marshals came to protect and guard us. The sorrow had been lifted, and we were able to keep marching toward a more just future. We believed that righteousness would always prevail in the end. We had to believe. There was no time for equivocating. The president demonstrated courage by protecting us. He didn't care what the political outcome would be. He didn't care if people disagreed. Courage can feel uncomfortable. Courage is not about being popular, it's about purpose.

There may be a time when history calls upon you. There may be an injustice that has hurt your friends or fellow citizens. How will you respond? Will you support those who are oppressed? By listening to the voice within, you will find the courage and power to do what is right, even if it is unpopular at the time. This inner courage will command you to respond to fighting with peace, and respond to hate with love.

ON CHARACTER

I think most humans are born with good character. You hear people speak of people with "good seeds." When people come into the world, they're born with a sense of completeness and wholeness. And for the most part, people remain that way. I believe that most people are kind and decent. They have good character and can tell the difference between right and wrong, and they have the will to choose. This is what Dr. King understood when he shared his dream that the day would come when we wouldn't be judged "by the color of our skin but by the content of our character." We all have free will. We can choose to be a force for truth and light. We can choose to have and to keep the strong character we were born with, to have strong mental and moral qualities. The choice is ours.

ON HUMILITY

Whatever good work you do, whatever powerful, profound work—do it because it's right or because it's necessary. Do it to make change for the better. Do it because you know you must. Don't do it for credit.

On Conscience

I came to Congress in 1987 with a reputation: that I was involved in the civil rights movement and was an advocate of nonviolence. I have spent my time in Congress continuing to practice what we preached during the movement. Sometimes that puts me at odds with those in my own party. But I'm okay with that because I am doing what is in my heart, what is in my conscience.

The Defense of Marriage Act in 1996 stipulated that marriage could only be between a man and a woman. I didn't think that was fair, and besides, what did marriage need saving from? From adultery or divorce? This law was designed to separate people who loved each other; it was meant to curtail and eliminate the freedoms of fellow Americans. So I voted against it.

You simply cannot tell people who they should love. There was a time in our country when people of different races couldn't be married. That was wrong then and it will always be wrong. Now we live in a time when people of different races can marry. Eventually, freedom and righteousness always prevail.

I always voted against that bill, which was signed into law by the president of my own party. I didn't lose any sleep over my decision because I knew I had to follow the dictates of my own heart. Here we are, decades later, and people of the same sexual orientation are permitted to marry whomever they choose. The Supreme Court has upheld that people of the same gender can get married. And that employers cannot discriminate against employees based on their orientation, who they love, or who they marry. These are victories for freedom, liberty, and equality.

I also voted against the 1994 crime bill that expanded the use of the death penalty. I couldn't in good conscience vote for something that sanctioned killing. We cannot and should not play

God. No government should get involved with this. There is divinity in each one of us, and when you kill someone, you are trying to do away with that spark. It is not right. I understand that the bill also increased funding for police systems. But I believe in nonviolence and believe we shouldn't kill people, even if they have done a wrong. I was conflicted about not supporting my party and president, and I would sometimes receive two hundred phone calls a day from constituents and others wanting to influence my vote. In the end, I listened to the voice within.

Listening to your conscience isn't easy. And it may make you deeply unpopular. Colin Kaepernick received widespread criticism when he decided to kneel during the national anthem in 2016, while he was the quarterback of the San Francisco 49ers. He was mocked and castigated. But he listened to the dictates of his heart. He followed his voice within. In the wake of the Black Lives Matter movement in 2020, many are seeing Kaepernick in a new light. They now say he was ahead of the curve, and that he was attuned to the racial inequality and police brutality that has gripped our nation. But I would say that he was following his conscience. He was living, as Dr. King would say, for something. You've got to be able to put everything on the line—your career, even your life—to help advance the rights and freedom of everyone.

ON HOPE

Never, ever lose hope. Never, ever give up. Keep the faith and be willing and ready to walk those last steps to help redeem our society. To move us closer to the creation of a loving community.

Hope is a feeling so deep in your heart, in the recesses of your body, that you know that good will triumph. It is a trust in the divine and the laws of the universe that things will work out as they should. It may be a long time coming, and you may not see it in your lifetime—or in that of your children or grandchildren. You must do all that you can during your time here to make things better and then pass the torch to the next generation.

When you have hope, you hold on to something so powerful that it almost wills it to happen. Hope also puts your mind at ease because you're putting your faith in a higher power.

Growing up, I had a teacher in elementary school who said, "Read, my child. Read." We only had a few books at home. My immediate family couldn't afford a subscription to the local newspaper, but my grandfather had one. After he got done reading it, I would go and read it. In 1956, when I was just sixteen years old, I went down to the Pike County Public Library in Troy, Alabama, with my siblings and cousins. I wanted to get a library card but was told that I couldn't because the cards were for whites only. I knew that it wasn't right or fair. I didn't get angry, upset, or bitter. I had hope that one day things would change.

Upon hearing Dr. Martin Luther King Jr. speak on the radio, I wrote him a letter. I didn't let my mother, father, or teachers know that I had written him. And he wrote me back and invited me to join him in Alabama. He called me "the Boy from Troy." I got involved in the movement and tried to play a humble role in helping right the wrongs that so many of my fellow brothers and sisters had faced. Throughout it all, I maintained hope.

The day eventually came when I could see my parents cast their first vote. The day eventually came when the "white" and "colored" signs of segregation came down. The day came when an African American was elected president of our great country. This is where hope can lead us.

The day even came when I wrote my autobiography, *Walking with the Wind*, and was invited back to the same library in Alabama to give a book talk. Hundreds of Black and white people came to listen. After I delivered my remarks, they gave me a library card. In 2013, after learning of my story, the public library in Troy, New York, presented me with a library card, too!

I have been criticized for being too hopeful, naïve, unrealistic. I still have hope left inside me. I have seen how a truth that only a few knew and believed has enveloped others. I have seen those who had hate in their hearts—who believed it was their mission to subjugate and segregate Black people—evolve into those who no longer harbor those feelings. They renounced their previously held views. They have asked for forgiveness for what they believed and how they have acted. They have seen the light. They became ambassadors for civil and human rights. And they now work to create a more peaceful and harmonious world by building bridges to communities that are in need of more understanding and empathy.

You may feel that you are alone. Or that you're the only one who believes so deeply in a cause that must be fully realized or advanced. But never, ever lose hope. Because when you lose hope, it means quitting on your brothers and sisters, on your friends and family, and on yourself.

ON SPIRITUALITY

I f there is one thing that I have learned in all my years, it is that transformation begins within. If you want to change the world and bring about a more peaceful society, you have to start with yourself. There is a battle that rages within. When you're angry, you're quick to fight, place blame, complain, and criticize.

If your inner life is in turmoil, how can you expect to radiate warmth and harmony in the world? How can you expect others to join you in your mission to heal the world? We all have to conquer the war within and understand that we are all children of God.

Spirituality is the focus on the human spirit over the material world. It calls for you to focus on the intrinsic qualities within you, and that which is good in the world. There is a divine spark in all of us that enables us to pause and observe our feelings so that we can act with more grace and dignity. We can be conscious participants in life. Instead of life happening *to* us, we can help move with a sense of purpose and mission.

I've found that praying daily has helped me to focus on and strengthen my spirituality. It helps me remember the virtues and good qualities of others. I pray and give thanks for the people and things in my life. This brings love, happiness, and serenity into my heart.

During the movement, we would drop to our knees and pray for the soul of our country. We prayed to awaken the divine spark of those who opposed us, so that they would realize we are all children of God. We prayed to awaken the spirit of bystanders, so that they too would realize that we are one family. We were in a struggle for preserving and strengthening the spirit of our country.

It can be difficult to lead a spiritual life because there are so many distractions of the material world. Distractions like fame, success, and money prevent us from listening to the voice within. We have to detach from the things we most want and what we most fear. This is when we will achieve divine enlightenment regarding our purpose. It's a daily battle. It's an internal battle. It's a necessary struggle.

ON FAITH

Faith is having complete trust and confidence in something or someone. Sometimes it means having trust in something you cannot see, touch, or feel. For that reason, faith can defy logic and reason. But that's even more reason to believe and keep the faith. Growing up in Alabama, I had faith that the world would eventually improve and become more equitable and just. I couldn't see it at the time, but I believed that it could and would happen.

You know, there are some stories I like to tell because they shaped who I am, and I never want to forget them. One is about growing up as the child of sharecroppers in rural Alabama. We considered everyone in our community to be like family. One weekend, about fifteen of us children in the community were playing in my aunt Seneva's yard, which was about half a mile from where I lived. What began as a sunny day turned into a dark one as the clouds gathered, turning the sky gray and moody. We heard the rumbling of thunder in the distance, and those sounds got closer and louder. The flash of lightning startled us as the sky was illuminated with bolts. I had seen firsthand what lightning could do—turning forests into fires. I was afraid of thunderstorms, their sounds, and the havoc they brought to our community. My mother would hush us whenever there was a thunderstorm, saying the Lord was doing His work.

Aunt Seneva gathered all of us children into her small house. We waited there quietly, listening to the rumblings, booms, and rolls outside. All of us children were afraid, and so was Aunt Seneva. The house began to rock from side to side. The floor beneath us started to buckle and arch. And then the roof above us started to lift. The storm was quite literally pulling the house up. Thinking quickly, Aunt Seneva told us to all hold hands and walk toward the corner of the room that was rising. This had the effect of weighing down this area of the house and keeping it grounded. When another corner began to lift, we walked to that corner as one to use our weight as a countervailing force. Wherever the house was rocked, we had faith in each other, that we could keep it under control, and that the higher power would protect us. We were walking with the wind.

I think this is a metaphor for how we live in the world today. Whenever the house of America is rocked or roiled by a problem or injustice, we have to join together as one, hold each other's hands, hold tight, and have faith that our collective and conscious action will secure this part of the house for the moment and for the future.

There are always storms. We have to walk in their direction. You see, marching is an act of faith. You have to trust that others will join you, and those who see and hear about the march will be reminded of our values and ideals. When there is a problem facing our land, we walk with the wind to redeem the soul of America. When there is a storm, there are those who walk to it and those who walk away. When you walk in its direction, you are demonstrating a moral force and showing that you have faith that everything works out as it should, and according to the will of the higher power.

The most frequent question that I get is "How did you do it? After getting beaten up, bloodied, and trampled upon, how did you not strike back or even try to defend yourself? How did you endure the death threats and abuses?"

My answer is: Faith.

I had faith in my heart that the fate of the world had already been written. And that my brothers and sisters and I in the movement were there to help bring that dream to reality. We believed that the dream already existed, and we had to invite others to share in its conception and manifestation. We were so sure about our convictions that we believed they were whispered into our hearts and minds by a higher power.

There's a reason that the movement began in the churches, and that reverends and churchgoers were integral. We were all people of faith. We were members of a community that relied on each other. We were believers.

We believed that humanity has a set of principles that are unshakable and unmovable. We believed that we are children of the Lord. Therefore, any type of discrimination or segregation was irrational and illogical. Why should the children be divided? We are one.

No matter how far we as a people or society stray from our moral compass, humans always have the capacity to return to our values. Our country has founding documents that enshrine our principles as life, liberty, and the pursuit of happiness. It's there in black and white. Yes, in black and white. The very writing of these words sealed the country's fate, that it would be a beacon for those in search of a better way of life. We in the movement had faith that Americans would want to live in keeping with their principles and not in conflict with them.

As difficult as it may seem today, with the killings of young Black people by the police, we have to keep faith that things will work out as they should, and in keeping with our principles and values. That doesn't mean that you should sit idly and watch events unfold. No, we must all be on the front lines, getting into good and necessary trouble. But when change doesn't happen in one day, or in one year, we can't lose faith that the day will come. Faith is inherent and intrinsic. It is what has given me peace, tranquility, and confidence, even in the darkest and dimmest moments in my life.

ON PATIENCE

I was just fourteen years old in 1954 when I learned that the Supreme Court had ruled that segregation was unconstitutional with the landmark decision *Brown v. Board of Education*.

I immediately believed that the next school year would go even better. For starters, it wouldn't be a segregated school. And I also had hopes that I wouldn't have to ride in a broken-down bus or use old books. Every day that I got on the bus, I kept expecting white children to join us. But it didn't happen. I realized that there was a disconnect between what I had heard on the radio and what was happening in my community. But I didn't grow angry or have despair. I didn't complain about my situation. I kept the faith and had patience that things would work out. If change wasn't going to happen to me and my community, I would respond to the call and help bring about the change.

When I was sixteen, I went to get my driver's license. I was scared, so I didn't do a very good job, and after the test the white official at the desk yelled, for everyone to hear, "Boy, don't you ever come here again unless you know how to drive." And I never went back. I didn't get my driver's license until I was forty-two. I was always with people, going from and to events, so I never had to be the driver. But I eventually got around to it. You don't have to do everything in a day. Take your time. Wait. Have patience. I had to learn to have patience. I didn't when I was a young man. You can go down every road in other ways. I did.

ON FEAR

B e unafraid.

Fear is a powerful and dangerous emotion. When I came of age, there was a real sense of fear among Black people. You could feel it just talking to people in the South. A Black person could get whisked away and never heard from again—or beaten in broad daylight. There were just too many stories like those of Emmett Till. While the overall situation has gotten better, we have so much further to go. These days there is an epidemic of police violence and brutality toward people of color. Black people are naturally fearful of what these government forces will do to them. Why should young Black people be guided by fear while they are making their way in the world, and why should parents have to bear the burden of fear of their children going out into the world?

In the movement, we faced our fears. We

would march and protest in broad daylight, with angry mobs and state troopers close by. But we kept on pushing and surviving. We got more exposure and experience. We learned about the people and ideas that we feared. And we realized that even if we were beaten or bruised, only we ourselves could determine whether we would be victims and suffer. That which we feared had no power over us, no hold whatsoever.

When you discover that your fears don't control you, that will be a moment of freedom and liberation. The key to getting over any fear is education and exposure. Why do you fear someone or something? What is it that you know about your fear? How could you learn more about it? Doing the work and gaining knowledge will make that which you fear more familiar. This is a moment of realization and transformation.

Think of something you fear. Now think through how you can learn more about it. Be bold, face it, practice and prepare for it, and you will realize you are stronger than you think you are.

The opposite of fear is freedom. We like to talk about freedom in America. But we also have a history of preventing people from being truly free. All too often we think that someone who is different from us should be denied freedoms. But we are all humans. We have so much in common, so much that is shared. It doesn't matter if someone is from another country far away, if someone looks different or sounds different. We all want the same things—to be free, to be able to take care of our family, and to do good. Don't let perceived differences be the source of fear. Get out there, learn, and overcome what you most fear so that you can be finally and truly free.

ON FORGIVENESS

The ability to forgive is one of the best quali-ties in a person. It can be difficult to forgive, to let go of your discontent, frustration, pride, and anger. As Dr. King often said, "Hate is too big a burden to bear." You need not shoulder the hurt or pain. Where there is forgiveness, there is the presence of a higher power.

When you forgive, you give yourself peace. You deserve this peace. By forgiving, you free yourself from negative thoughts and from spiral-ing downward. This is when you can start the healing process and move toward reconciliation. An apology may never come. But it may. And when it does: Forgive.

Only once did someone apologize for attacking me. I was beaten up, bloodied, and bruised after the Freedom Ride to Rock Hill, South Carolina, in 1961. Some fifty years later, I was contacted by Elwin Wilson, a former member of the Ku Klux Klan. He was one of our assailants, and he made it a point to apologize to Freedom Riders in ceremonies. He came to Washington, DC, with his son to apologize in person. He told me, "I am sorry about what I did that day. Will you forgive me?" I accepted his apology. We hugged and cried together. He had grown to see what was decent and right. He told me that he wanted to "make right" before meeting his Maker, and I believed he did just that.

I didn't need him to apologize to forgive him. Because I had long ago decided that I wasn't going to be bound by the mental shackles of hate, anger, and discontent. Forgiveness is medicine for the mind, balm for the body, and healing for the heart.

In 2009 Peggy Wallace Kennedy, the daughter of former Alabama governor George Wallace— who vowed segregation—marched with me across the Edmund Pettus Bridge [in Alabama, where police attacked peaceful demonstrators seeking voting rights for African Americans in 1965]. She wanted to show solidarity. She felt bad and wanted to change the trajectory from that day and her father's vow in 1963. I told her we can. We can move on. It's time. That's reconciliation. That's making your own way.

I hope that forgiveness can become a greater part of our national character. Everyone makes mistakes, and we are so quick to rush to judgment and cast aspersions. Where is forgiveness and mercy in the public arena? If we formed policy based on mercy, we would have a stronger and more equal justice system and a more equitable economy. For example, the House of Representatives passed a resolution that apologized for slavery [in 2008]. We should also pass resolutions that state our apologies for the death and wars we have created.

We shouldn't create policy that is based on fear, revenge, and retribution. If we were quicker to forgive, we would create a more empathetic world where we heal and rehabilitate people—not penalize them. Forgiveness is profound. And it is a way forward—but first you must get out of your own way and allow for healing.

ON HAPPINESS

Written into the Declaration of Independence is "the Pursuit of Happiness." A country cannot be independent or happy if it is subjugating and oppressing others. The assailant is full of hate, and the victim is full of fear. Neither is happy, independent, or free. Our work in the civil rights movement was an effort to make America live up to the ideals enshrined in its founding documents. When we rid our country of racism, oppression, and inhumanity, we are able to live more freely and more happily. This is a constant challenge—to pursue happiness. When we move with love and work toward peace, we're on the path to happiness as people, as a country, and as a world.

Happiness is the essence of life. When you're happy, you're at your best. Don't underestimate the power of a kind, warm smile. Sometimes I smile at myself, sometimes at others. It always lifts my spirits. A smile is a gift. Laughter is a gift. It takes very little to uplift others. You can always give someone a positive experience of being in your presence and radiating warmth.

You don't have to deny yourself happiness and pleasure. There is joy in searching for the truth, in finding what matters to you, and helping improve the world so that it is a more peaceful place. I am happiest when I am in service to others. When you lose yourself in service to others, you will find purpose and fulfillment. There you will find happiness.

I like to dance. There's a video of me in the office clapping and snapping along to the Pharrell Williams song "Happy," from the movie *Despicable Me 2*. I was also filmed dancing to the same song at a campaign event in Georgia. Now people like playing that tune when I go places. And I try to oblige with my dancing, moving my hips and having fun. It's my song. Dancing is my body's way of manifesting happiness. Movement.

Strawberry and vanilla milk shakes and orange chicken make me happy. Having an occasional Diet Coke also gives me pleasure. The Coca-Cola Company, which is based in Atlanta, furnishes Coca-Cola products to all members of the Georgia delegation. And these drinks are made available to our staff, constituents, and guests. Georgia also farms a lot of peanuts. So the Georgia Peanut Commission provides us peanuts to give to guests, too. But I don't eat them because I grew up eating peanuts, and I don't want to eat them anymore. When I'm on a plane and the flight attendant offers me peanuts, I usually decline.

Happiness is being at home after a long day, playing with and feeding my cats.

I'm a happy person.

ON FRIENDSHIP

A friend asks you how are you doing. They want to know where you are in your life journey. They don't judge or evaluate. They listen with an empathetic ear and try to be a sounding board. A friend doesn't give up on you. They are with you through thick and thin. They don't expect anything in return. Your presence is enough. Friends can agree or agree to disagree. A friend can share a truth even when it's hard and can hurt. True friendships don't weaken or waver. There is hope and love between friends, a connection between spirits and souls. Everyone needs a friend to walk on the path together.

On Love

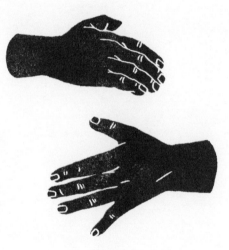

There are many types of love. Love for your family, for your parents, children, and spouse. There is love for God and the divine. That means having faith that righteousness will prevail and the path will unfold according to the Almighty's plan.

It's not popular to talk about love, and some think it's naïve. We're afraid to say "I love you," and we almost never talk about love in Congress or in public forums. It's as if people think love is a sign of weakness, vulnerability, and emotionality. But love can be strong. It can be binding. Love is a force unlike any other. I hope we can get to a place where saying "I love you" is a badge of honor.

I believe love means that you're willing to sacrifice, to go to the ends of the earth for someone. Love was the engine of the civil rights movement.

I risked death for love. I know that this isn't the conventional view.

We cared not only about those who were marching with us but those who opposed us. Every human being is deserving and worthy of being loved. Our goal was to achieve unity. There's a quote of Dr. King's that I use from time to time, which I rephrase: "To be bold, to be creative, to never give up, and never to hate—for hate is too big a burden to bear. I have decided to love."

After the marches, protests, and struggle, there would be a time for reconciliation and harmony. When we marched, we walked in peace, without hate, and with love. It was a nonviolent revolution. You may hit me, you may beat me, you may unleash your dogs on me and almost kill me. But I am still going to love you. As Dr. King would tell us, "Just love 'em."

I never stop trying to impress upon people that children are not born with hate in their hearts. Nobody comes into the world with distrust and anger toward people who are different from them. They are taught to feel and act a certain way. Children learn from their surroundings and acquire their sentiments and beliefs over time. Children can also learn to love others. And so, we all have the capacity to revisit our beliefs and biases and love one another. We can all grow in the direction of love.

Are you able to love someone who doesn't like you? Can you love someone who has wronged you? When you open your heart to someone, you are demonstrating your abundant spirit and sharing your self-worth. Only you have the power over your mind and your heart.

ON MARRIAGE

For the early part of my life, I was married to the movement, and I didn't have time to take my personal life into consideration. There wasn't a lot of time for intimate relationships, as we were always so busy with the work itself. I was constantly in meetings and traveling across the South. We were in the middle of the struggle to redeem the soul of America. And it just wasn't on our minds. We were too busy trying to survive.

Marriage is one of the most important decisions that you will make. You have to choose wisely because this is the person who will be with you in those quiet moments when there is nobody else. Find someone with whom you're compatible and with whom you're a friend. Someone who listens to you and cares about you for who you are. Someone you can grow with and has your best interests at heart—and someone who has your back. At the same time, give a little space and don't suffocate your partner.

The secret to a good, long, healthy marriage is love, unconditional love. It's being there for your spouse through both the good and challenging times.

I met my late wife, Lillian, at a New Year's Eve party in 1967. We got married the very next year. She was a librarian at Atlanta University. She was a very smart woman who was knowledgeable about the world, and she read widely. She and I used to go on double dates with our friends Julian and Alice Bond [Julian Bond, like Lewis, was one of the founders of the Student Nonviolent Coordinating Committee]. Lillian had also been involved in politics as an activist. We shared that in common. She was also an educator and worked closely with young people, nurturing them as they grew into young adults and the leaders of our next generation. She was a delegate to the Democratic National Convention in 1972. She encouraged me to run for Congress in 1977, which I did but lost. And she was there to comfort me. She was integral to my life in every way. She made me laugh. That is key to a good partnership. And she was the life of a party. She was even good-natured about driving me around all those years when I didn't have my license!

She was warm and giving, she was a beautiful mother—and I miss her.

ON LEARNING

We didn't just show up and march. We had training and we developed a plan. We studied intently the philosophy of nonviolence. Like any discipline that you try to master, you need to constantly train, practice, and enhance your skills. If you want to learn an instrument, you have to spend time in the practice room working on your technique. When it came to understanding and practicing the nonviolent philosophy, we had to learn how *not* to respond to anything that made us angry, upset, or bitter. We had to learn how not to be provoked.

We relied on many great teachers to help us learn and adopt the practice of nonviolence. When I was a student at Fisk University in Nashville, Tennessee, I would join with other students at a humble Methodist church downtown. There were students from Vanderbilt, Peabody College,

Tennessee State. We would listen to our teacher Jim Lawson, who was a conscientious objector during the Korean War. Many have referred to Lawson as the "mystic of the movement." He was a mentor to many of us at the Student Nonviolent Coordinating Committee (SNCC). He had traveled to India as a Methodist missionary to walk in the footsteps of Gandhi. He was a contemporary and friend of Dr. King, who urged him to move to the South.

Lawson was our teacher. He shared with us the wisdom, writings, and philosophies of Gandhi, Tolstoy, Thoreau, Aristotle, Plato. He walked us through examples of how Gandhi had *satyagraha*, which is a type of truth force and nonviolent resistance.

Lawson guided us to observe the world around us and, most important, to observe ourselves in it. When you stop and notice your own reactions and responses, you can manage them. It starts with being aware and conscious of your own thoughts.

During our training, we even had role-playing and drama sessions in which we would act out scenarios that we might encounter during our protests. For example, we would have a group of Black and white students simulate what it would be like to be intimidated, harassed, and spit on. We sat at counters and someone would yell at us, call us names, and even pour cold water on us. We wanted the experience to feel real, so that when it happened out in the world, we would be better prepared. In the real world, we had hot coffee and hot chocolate poured on us. Cigarettes were put out in our hair. We were knocked to the ground, and we got right back up and sat on the stool at the lunch counter.

There were many discussions about how to respond if violently attacked, and we developed best practices. If you were knocked over, you should roll up into a ball, and protect your head and the most sensitive parts of your body. It was important to look out for each other, in case someone needed immediate medical attention. We always tried to maintain eye contact with our attackers because that meant sending a message that "I am still human. And so are you." When you look your assailant in the eye, you level the playing field because you envelop them in your humanity, and you may get them to find some empathy. We even encouraged protesters to smile—not to be smug, but to be decent and polite. And always to be nonviolent.

We were taught to see our attackers in a new light. Think of them as recently born babies. They surely weren't born with hate in their hearts. What went wrong in their lives to bring them to the moment that they are in today? Was there something insufficient in their upbringing? Did they lack the emotional support at home? Did someone teach this child to hate and abuse others? Don't give up on your assailants. Try to understand them. It's not easy, and it takes considerable work.

We received detailed and inspirational wisdom from our teachers like Reverend Lawson. I think that's what we should look for in our teachers today. Those who put their students first and prepare them for what they will encounter in the real world. The more you can simulate what you're going to experience, the more you will be prepared for what the world throws at you.

ON ART

I always wished I could paint and draw. Or take beautiful photographs. One of my friends during the movement was Danny Lyon. I've known him for over fifty years. He was the photographer of the Student Nonviolent Coordinating Committee [SNCC]. He was my roommate in Atlanta, and he used the bathroom as the darkroom to develop his pictures. Sometimes I would go into the bathroom and I would be nervous that I would pick up the wrong thing to brush my teeth. We don't talk for long stretches of time, but when we meet, we pick up right where we left off. I like looking at his photographs of the movement because they take me back to moments where we formed our bonds of being brothers and sisters.

We did a lot of singing during the movement, but I am definitely not a singer.

Mahalia Jackson is one of my favorite singers.

She sang "How I Got Over" at the March on Washington in 1963, and it's a song that stays with me to this day. I hear the music in my heart and lyrics in my mind: "I wanna sing hallelujah, I'm gonna shout all my trouble over..." Some of the musicians I enjoyed listening to back in the day include Curtis Mayfield, Solomon Burke, Mavis Staples, Betty Peebles, and Lou Rawls. I also like Barbra Streisand, Jennifer Hudson, John Legend, Usher, and Jennifer Holliday.

Growing up, I saw a few movies, mostly Westerns like *The Lone Ranger* and *Billy the Kid*. I remember watching *Tarzan*, too. But I didn't enjoy going to the theater because "colored" people like me had to sit in the balcony. Even to this day, I don't go out to see many movies at the theater because it reminds me of that experience when I was a kid.

It's through literature, poetry, music, and film that we can share insights and truths with new audiences. Art softens the heart and mind so that you can appeal to the better angels of those who are reading, listening, and watching your work. Art brings us all together because it is a reminder of our common humanity.

If you're not an artist yourself, you can still support the arts by being a patron. My late friend Ambassador Anne Cox Chambers was a patron and benefactor to many artists. She bought many original paintings from Benny Andrews, a prominent African American artist from Georgia, and donated them to the National Center for Civil and Human Rights in Atlanta. Her generosity allowed for more people to see and experience these great paintings. You can always do what you can to support artists and help to make the world a more beautiful place in which to live for all of us.

I'm glad that we built the National Museum of African American History and Culture [NMAAHC]. Growing up, my teachers told me to cut out pictures in magazines of prominent

African Americans who we admired for Negro Week (we didn't have African American History Month back then). I found pictures of George Washington Carver and Jackie Robinson. Now we have a museum [the NMAAHC, part of the Smithsonian and supported by Lewis, opened in 2016] that will enshrine these incredible figures and so many more for posterity. This museum is the realization of a dream that began over one hundred years ago, when African American veterans of World War I gathered at the Nineteenth Street Baptist Church to discuss ways to commemorate the contributions of their community. I hope that all who visit the museum on the National Mall are deeply inspired by what they see and experience. Let it be a beacon to children, ministers, revolutionaries, and all who want to participate in our democracy.

We need artists and writers now to help create more empathy in the world. To teach us what we may not yet know, to take us on adventures, to share points of view. To learn about history and read our stories—so that we can never forget. To make us laugh and to bring us to tears. We need to make books available to children so they can easily learn about the world, and they can follow their imaginations. Children who read maintain their sense of wonder and ask questions—necessary questions—that make us examine why things are the way they are. And adults are ever learning. I know I am. I know what I don't know and that I am forever thirsty for knowledge.

ON BOOKS

I liked reading comic books when I was a young adult. I read *Martin Luther King and the Montgomery Story*. It cost ten cents. This powerful use of imagery and text brought Dr. King's message to young people. The book was distributed among young Black and white people who were interested in what was happening in the South. It became the guide for many students in Tennessee and North Carolina on what to do and how to act in a nonviolent manner. More recently I did the *March* trilogy, about my journey in the movement. I went to Comic-Con and that was fun, especially talking to the kids. I enjoyed meeting so many people who love comic books, too. I've written a few books, as you know.

One of my few hobbies has been going to flea markets and searching for old posters and books. I like going to Weschler's [an auction house]. I am a history buff. Both my homes, in Atlanta and Washington, DC, are crammed with books and old artifacts. Some of the authors that I enjoy reading include Frederick Douglass and Booker T. Washington. I especially enjoy the poetry of Langston Hughes and Maya Angelou.

My favorite book is a first edition that I found in a flea market in Alexandria, Virginia. It's *Stride Toward Freedom*, by Martin Luther King Jr. There was a Sunday service program stuck in its pages that was dated June 21, 1960. And the book was inscribed "Best Wishes, Martin Luther King Jr." I thought they were going to charge me an arm and a leg for the book, but it only cost fifty cents. I keep the book locked in a safe in Atlanta, and it's one of the most valuable things that I own. I never really saved anything from my time with Dr. King. I didn't think he would be slain while he was young. I thought we would grow old together and would have time to reminisce. Dr. King had given me a signed copy of his *Where Do We Go From Here* in 1964, but it went missing from my office.

My favorite book? I always, *always*, return to Scripture.

ON SPORTS

S ports are a wonderful way to build bridges in a community. Fans forget about their political leanings, and they put aside their differences to support a common goal. I wish we could draw more inspiration from sports teams in the halls of Congress. We are all on one team. We are all Americans.

I admired Muhammad Ali. He gave up his career to stand up for what he believed. This took real courage and character. He spoke out against the Vietnam War, which was an unjust and unnecessary war, and decided not to serve. My father and uncles always rooted for Ali because his victories were victories for African Americans, showing that our community could excel and outperform.

I was overjoyed when the Atlanta United FC won the Major League Soccer championship. It was a great victory for the city of Atlanta. It helped to bring more happiness, joy, and goodwill to our city. I was also so proud that Atlanta hosted the Olympic Games in 1996. And I'm a longtime fan of the Atlanta Braves.

ON DRESS

Growing up, I would try to look my best in school. I always thought I would become a preacher, and my teachers and people around town called me "boy preacher."

When I was seventeen, I was going to participate in my first sit-in. We always wanted to look our best during the protests, so that we presented a strong image of being courteous and professional. Folks would wear their Sunday best clothes during the sit-ins and protests.

I bought myself a secondhand suit at a thrift store because I didn't have much money. There was a barbershop in the back, so I got myself a haircut, too. I wanted to look fresh and sharp. My hair was naturally curly, and I would put some water in there to make it look shinier. I used to have sideburns and a mustache, too.

Throughout my career in Congress, people

often confused me for my dear friend Elijah Cummings. I thought about growing a beard so people could tell us apart. I even told Elijah that I was going to get a tattoo on the back of my head so that no one would confuse us—and he laughed.

I believe that when you're clean and fresh, you are prepared to take on the struggles ahead of you. When you are neat and tidy, your mind will be uncluttered.

I wear ties. I used to shop for clothes at Rich's in downtown Atlanta and at Nordstrom's. For much of my career, I had something of a uniform—a blue suit that I wore as a congressman.

ON MONEY

I return to Scripture when it says: "For what shall it profit a man, if he should gain the whole world, but lose his soul?" (Mark 8:36).

I grew up poor. And I've never really had much money to my name. After I got married, I was making a small salary while serving on the city council, and my wife was working at the library. Our only significant asset was our house. My wife's friends gave her a hard time for marrying me because I didn't make much money.

Accumulating money has never been a goal of mine. But when I see injustices that concern money, I stand up and speak out. Dr. King said that Black Americans had been given a check but it was marked "insufficient funds." Black people today continue to have a difficult time accessing capital, education, and opportunities.

How a country spends its money reflects its

priorities and values. We spend billions of dollars on wars and in other countries. How about we use that money here at home building schools, to feed the hungry, for housing and medical facilities? We are a rich and bountiful nation. We can do so much more by making smart investments here, raising the minimum wage, and assuring equal pay for everyone—no matter your ethnicity, gender, orientation, or any perceived difference.

I also support putting more women and people of color on our currency. We should put Harriet Tubman, Sojourner Truth, Eleanor Roosevelt, and Dr. Martin Luther King Jr. on our money. This would have the effect of reminding everyone about our values and principles. We would be honoring those who made our country stronger and more prosperous. The images of these individuals would help inspire young people to learn their stories, and in this way these images can help to shape the future of our country.

ON IMMIGRATION

There is no such thing as an "illegal human." America is a country that is composed of immigrants and their descendants. They are part of the very fabric of our nation.

Immigrants touch all parts of life in America. Our universities attract the most promising and brightest minds from all over the world. Immigrants are healers who serve as doctors, nurses, and medical staff in communities across our nation. They are entrepreneurs who start companies that create jobs that serve as the engine for the economy. They defend our country by serving in the armed services. They serve in leadership positions at all levels, from the local to the federal.

I say to immigrants: Welcome home. America wants and needs you. We want your creativity, your fresh outlooks, your ideas, and your contributions to make our country and world a better place. What makes America special is that we respect our differences—and we are better when we listen to and grow with each other.

The immigration status of someone shouldn't be used to discriminate against them or withhold proper treatment. There are too many ways in which immigrants and their children are denied freedom, equality, and basic rights in our country. And to separate parents from their babies: Never, ever. Human cages: Never, ever.

My ancestors came here as slaves four hundred years ago against their will. And now we're telling people of color that they can't come here any-more. This has the stench of racism. Call it what it is. Put the cards on the table.

"Dreamers," those brought to the United States by their parents, have been treated like a political football. They've been told to leave the country and are living with great anxiety and uncertainty about their status as Americans.

I support legislation that creates a pathway

for Dreamers to remain here—in their homes as Americans. They are already Americans in all but paperwork. They are friends, neighbors, cousins, brothers, and sisters. I also support legislation that prohibits states from denying the opportunity for Dreamers to study at institutions of higher learning. For example, my home state of Georgia doesn't let Dreamers attend the University of Georgia or Georgia Tech. Immigrants have rights, and we have an imperative to treat them with dignity, decency, and respect. It makes no sense at all to have so many people living in the shadows.

We do not need to build walls between Americans. We also don't need to build walls between our neighbors. When Dr. Martin Luther King Jr. visited Berlin in 1964, he reminded those at the wall that it couldn't deny the fact that we're all brothers and sisters, children of God. Building a wall on our southern border is a similar exercise. How can we separate ourselves from God's children? We cannot allow the construction of a wall, this monument of intolerance and ineptitude. Just as we are taking down the monuments of the Confederacy, we don't need to create another symbol of division.

ON ORIENTATION

Y ou should be free to love whomever you want. Follow what is in your heart. Let people be who they want to be. And nobody should be the victim of discrimination on account of sexual orientation.

I have to admit that even those in leadership positions within the civil rights movement struggled with this. Bayard Rustin was one of the best intellects in the movement. There was a long debate regarding whether he should be the chair of the March on Washington. Some leaders thought he wasn't the best choice because he was openly gay. They didn't want Southern senators to oppose the march, the movement, and potential legislation that was being proposed. After much discussion, Dr. King, James Farmer [a cofounder of the Congress of Racial Equality who organized the first Freedom Ride], and I came to the conclusion to appoint A. Philip Randolph [a prominent civil rights leader] to be the chair, with the understanding that Rustin would be appointed as deputy. Rustin basically organized the entire march, from the logistics of getting people there to the flow of the event. He received the Presidential Medal of Freedom in 2013.

We have to keep working every day to examine our biases. And to let people be free to follow their conscience. Every human being should be able to live in a world free from fear and hate. Black lives matter. Black LGBTQ+ lives matter.

Everyone deserves to be respected and treated with dignity. There is more work to do to help my brothers and sisters in this community gain their freedom and live without fear of reprisal.

I'm always honored and happy to march in the Atlanta Pride Parade. It gives me pleasure to see so many of my brothers and sisters marching in solidarity and advocating for the fair treatment of all.

ON THE
ENVIRONMENT

We must save the planet. We must save it for generations yet unborn. We only pass this way once. We have a moral obligation to do what we can to preserve and save this little piece of real estate in the universe that we call Earth. Let us do all that we can to make sure the air is clean, the water is pure, and the ecosystems are healthy. Mother Nature provides us the nutrients to subsist, from the womb to old age. We must also take care of her, as she is the giver of all life.

Our planet is in trouble as we continue to release dangerous chemicals into the atmosphere and into the water. There are powerful hurricanes that have grown in severity and have impacted places like Puerto Rico and Mozambique. At the same time, cutting down the forests in Brazil and Indonesia increases the amount of greenhouse gases here. We're all connected. The pesticides used in one part of the world would impact yet another area miles and even continents away.

We have to act before it's too late. Let's take climate change seriously. We can and must make the planet safer, greener, and cleaner than when we inherited it. Our children and grandchildren deserve to inherit a planet that is healthy and beautiful, so they can live in communion with nature. We cannot prioritize the short-term profit of corporations over the sanctity of the place in which we live and the giver of life, Mother Nature. In order for humanity to survive, we need to do everything we can to take care of our planet.

There are many steps we can take as individuals to help the environment. We can bike regularly, take public transportation to work, and recycle our paper, cans, and bottles. And there is so much more we must do and can do, including holding corporations to a much higher standard, making sure they are accountable.

We also have to respect the creatures on the planet. These days we don't have much of a connection to animals other than what is served on our plates. Growing up, I lived on a farm and was around animals. I was responsible for raising the chickens. You know that about me. I would mark the first egg that was laid with a pencil. And then I would have to wait for weeks for it to hatch. Meanwhile, the hens would move around, so I had to know which egg is which. Sometimes I would cheat on the sitting hens and move their eggs and hatchlings around. No, it wasn't the most moral, loving, and nonviolent thing to do. But that was our method of raising chickens. This helped me to pay attention and appreciate the animals with which we share this world.

I have cats at home in Washington, DC, and they remind me that we as humans are not alone on our planet.

ON COVID-19

The outbreak of COVID-19 is a global tragedy. I am saddened that so many lives have been cut short by this virus. My thoughts and prayers are with the families, loved ones, and friends who are grieving those who are no longer with us.

Many other countries have been able to "flatten the curve." Yet here in the United States, there is debate and politicization over whether to take necessary precautions, like wearing a mask or socially distancing. Why create divisiveness? This makes no sense. This is anti-science. Our country is supposed to be a leader in science. The pandemic is a national humiliation.

We need to remember that we live together as brothers and sisters in an American House— a Global House. What happens in the Southern states affects the Northern states. What happens in the Western Hemisphere can affect the Eastern Hemisphere. Let's also not scapegoat Asians and Asian Americans for this illness. We live in a global, interconnected, diverse, and multicultural world.

It is clear that we must make every effort to protect the health of everyone affected by the pandemic, especially those most at risk, such as the elderly and people of color. The outbreak has revealed the inequalities of our health care system, as those who have the means are able to receive testing and treatment more quickly. Every life is deserving and worthy of care. There shouldn't be winners and losers when it comes to accessing proper treatment. We are one people and can take care of everyone.

Our country needs a national plan that responds to the pandemic. We have a mandate to act. We need to speak with one voice and follow the guidance of health professionals. Every minute, every second we wait—costs lives.

This is a biological threat that knows no borders, area codes, or zip codes. We're all in this together, as humanity is being tested. We can work with our allies to share best practices and create a global response to mitigate the havoc this terrible virus has brought upon so many.

We owe a debt of gratitude to the doctors, nurses, administrators, and all who are on the front lines healing us. We also are grateful to the researchers and medical experts who are working on the cure that will put this pandemic behind us. We need to be investing now in the manufacturing and distribution capabilities for an eventual vaccine.

During the quarantine, we have seen just how important essential workers are. We can't take them for granted. Thank you to the delivery people, postal workers, sanitation workers, food preparers, educators, and numerous others who are working diligently to keep us safe and secure during these challenging times.

There is no place or time for complacency or indifference. This is real. As real as any enemy. Let us not lose hope or be consumed with despair. As dark as it may seem right now, there will be better days ahead. We must keep the faith.

ON HEALTH CARE

I have tried to take my health seriously through-out my life. While in Congress, I have tried to work out every morning in the gym. I also walk through the long corridors, so I get my steps in every day. These days I am fighting an illness and trying to manage my health and diet as much as I can. I am doing as well as I can. I draw inspiration from President Jimmy Carter, who prevailed against cancer, and so have many others fighting this disease.

I believe that health care is a human right. We have to take every measure and step to take care of the health of everyone. All too often there are stigmas around certain diseases and illnesses. In years past, I have made it a point to get an HIV/AIDS test to show that we representatives in Congress can also be affected by this disease. We have made tremendous progress in treating, preventing, and fighting this. If you have this disease, I want you to know that you are still loved, appreciated, and cherished. We are here fighting with and for you.

When it comes to public health, every leader has the responsibility of educating and communicating with the public about appropriate steps to take. This helps reduce stigmas and enhances awareness among the public. We need change so that there is better health care. No gaps. Every family can be taken care of in our American house.

ON VISION

When I was just eleven years old, in 1951, I traveled with my family from rural Alabama to Buffalo, New York, to visit relatives. It was the first time I had left the South. The trip helped me see things differently. My relatives in Buffalo lived next to a white family, and it was the first time I saw Blacks and whites living as neighbors and as friends. I saw an escalator and elevator for the first time. I saw people moving up and down with speed. And they were moving together as Blacks and whites and as Americans.

I realized that the world was bigger than Alabama, and there were people who thought and acted differently from those where I lived. When we got back to Alabama, my cousins and I tried to saw down a large pine tree so that we could make a bus out of the wood and roll out of the state and escape.

Going to Buffalo was when I realized that we live in one house as Americans and as humans in this world. I started to believe that we were all connected. It was a vision of what we were and could become. If one part of the house starts to rot or the roof has a leak, then the entire house is in jeopardy. A damaged house is bad for everyone. You have to take care of the house, to make sure everything is in order and functioning properly.

Having a vision is powerful. It means believing what you see and feel, and then bringing those visions into reality. It's hard work, too. When you visualize something, you need to have faith that you'll get there. The day will come that your vision will be realized.

Eventually, our vision of living in one house did materialize with the passage of significant civil and voting rights legislation. There is more to do. There always is. We can't get complacent or sit on the sidelines. We aren't just Southerners and

Northerners. We have to make people everywhere understand that we already live in one house and that we ought to act to protect where we live. It doesn't matter your race, ethnicity, heritage, orientation. We are one.

Vision is the opposite of ignorance, and our vision is unity.

ON
COMMUNICATION

I moved to Atlanta after college and attended the church where Dr. Martin Luther King Jr. preached. While he was practicing his sermons, his father—Daddy King—would sit in the first pew and say, "Make it plain. Make it clear. Make it real." And Dr. King would do just that, using clear and simple language to communicate his message.

I drew inspiration from Daddy King's advice. I have given many speeches over my time. And when I draft a speech, or speak with unprepared remarks, I use simple language. But I also use powerful words that will speak directly to those in the audience. There is no mistaking where I stand when I talk. I try to speak with conviction and confidence.

What is it that you want to say? How can you boil it down to the fewest words? What is the central truth that you're trying to communicate? You don't have to use fancy words to impress people. You don't need to have an advanced degree or be an impressive speechwriter. When you speak with conviction and emotion, you will appeal to the hearts of your listeners. Your message will resonate with them. It's what you are saying that matters and endures.

It's okay to be bold and push the envelope when you're pushing for justice and liberty. At the March on Washington in 1963, I had a line in the prepared remarks that was a provocative question: "I want to know, which side is the federal government on?" This was a simple, plain, and real question that got to the heart of the matter. Would the federal government be on the side of justice, liberty, and basic decency, as so many of us were marching for our rights? Or would the powers that be watch idly and do nothing? For doing nothing and saying nothing is being complicit in the situation, and denying the rights of so many. As with my other line about marching through the South like Sherman [see "On Activism"], I was told to remove the line because it might come across as too direct and threatening. After all, we were trying to win the support of the federal government, not antagonize and scare it away.

Yes, we have to choose our words carefully. Maybe it's not the right time to say a certain phrase or put something a certain way. But it's never the right time to say nothing and to stay silent. We all have the obligation to communicate with each other about the type of society and world in which we want to live. This could be speaking with friends, writing a paper or post, or giving a speech to members of your community so that people know where you stand. When you get out there and communicate what is in your heart, you will inspire many more to speak up and out about what is in theirs. Every movement is about communication, and how we choose to communicate is integral to the direction and eventual success of the movement.

You can also communicate with actions to draw attention to that which you are protesting or demonstrating against. During the civil rights movement, we dramatized certain events so that they would invite attention and press coverage. We would time our marches so they coincided with the news. In fact, the news anchor on ABC had to interrupt the movie *Judgment at Nuremberg*, about the trials of Nazis after World War II, to share word of the Bloody Sunday protests in Selma, Alabama, in 1965.

Most of all, communicate your authentic self.

The media likes to cover conflict, and we took this into consideration as we thought about where to protest and how to organize. Mind you, we didn't ever want to get into a physical conflict with those who opposed us. We were in a moral conflict with the laws of our country and how we were treated. Our quarrel wasn't with individuals but the institutions that kept us down for so many years. When we did indeed march, we did so peacefully. But that provoked the powers that be, as we were bringing to the foreground the terrible moral transgressions in our society.

You can't communicate in a vacuum. You have to think carefully, not only about the message you're trying to send, but how you're going to send it. During the movement, there was the radio, a few television shows, and the print media. These days there are so many options, and Americans are saturated with choices on where and how to consume their information. You have your phones and social media 24/7.

However, I am convinced that if you tell the truth and speak from your heart, your message will shine through, no matter the outlet. You will be able to touch people by your actions, as actions speak much louder than words. When other people are talking about problems, you're out there taking action, getting into good trouble, and doing something about it.

Always remember what Daddy King said: "Make it plain. Make it clear. Make it real." Speak the language of the people. And make sure to understand with whom you are communicating. Who are they? What are their values? What are their needs? Your job as a communicator is to figure all that out and apply that knowledge to what you are saying.

ON VOTING

VOTE VOTE VOTE VOTE VOTE. Write that in capital letters in your notes. All over the page. Remember the time when the right to vote was denied us? I do. And once we could vote, there were lines and lines and lines to register. We can't afford to let democracy slip away. We fought for that right. Demonstrated with bandages on our heads. We fought to prevent changes to the Voting Rights Act and then to restore it. We were weary, tired, but we had purpose. Don't take this right for granted. Don't squander it. Keep building. A vote is your voice being heard. A vote is your power. A vote is your change. A vote is sacred.

Go out there and VOTE.

ON DEATH

I don't fear death. I've faced death before.

I was prepared to die in 1961. I was just twenty-one years old when I, along with six other Blacks and six whites, left Washington, DC, on a Greyhound bus headed to New Orleans. We wanted to test a Supreme Court decision that prohibited segregation in interstate transportation. We had learned and internalized the philosophy of nonviolence before embarking upon this Freedom Ride. As I got off the bus in Rock Hill, South Carolina, I heard: "Other side, nigger." I was immediately knocked to the floor and was kicked and punched by irate men. We were left bloody and bruised. When the police asked whether we wanted to press charges, we declined. As I've pointed out, our struggle wasn't against individuals but the institution of racism and injustice.

I was prepared to die one day in Selma, Alabama. I had a backpack with a couple of books and fruit in it because I thought the police would arrest me and I wanted to have something to eat and read while I was in jail. I saw the legion of Alabama state troopers across that bridge [the Edmund Pettus Bridge, over the Alabama River on the road to Montgomery]. The police said, "We'll give you three minutes to disperse and return to your homes or to your church." The co-leader of the march, Hosea Williams, responded: "Major, give us a moment to kneel and pray."

But the police didn't wait. They started moving toward us with such force. They ran me over and beat me with sticks over the head. I thought that maybe my time had come. I thought I would die right there on the bridge. There was a certain peace in this realization. I was unafraid. If it was my time to die, I knew that my sacrifice would mean something, and it would not be in vain. I would have given my life to the cause which was greater than myself. That was my love to give, too. My life had a purpose, even if that meant giving it to help improve the lives of others. Dr. King once said that if we don't have a cause or purpose for which we're willing to die, then we're not fit to live.

Life and death are linked. What truth do you believe so strongly that you're willing to die for it? When you let go of your fears, you will find meaning and life in the service of others.

ON LEAVING
A LEGACY

I would like to be remembered as a boy from Troy, Alabama, who saw something, said something, and did something about it. I hope that those who learn my story are inspired to take action in their communities. To push, to pull, to fight for the rights of all people. It's important to never lose hope and to realize that in the end, what matters was how you treated people, whether you were kind to them, and how you responded to the wrongs that you or your brothers and sisters faced. Every generation leaves behind a legacy. I am one of the last of mine. I am going to be passing the torch. These fierce young people protesting, marching, standing up, and sitting in are like I was.

ON THE FUTURE

We have made progress over the past many decades. Dr. King and the civil rights movement birthed a committed new generation of activists who are imagining, envisioning, and shaping the world they want to see.

One hundred years from now, I would love to see that our Beloved Community, the place we call home—America—will be more at peace with itself. Let us hope and believe that there will be less turmoil, less rancor, less violence. America should be a place of respect and dignity, a beacon of light for all of our fellow human beings. I know it is within our power to make such a world exist.

Be patient. Be hopeful. Be humble. Be bold. Be better.

Keep the faith.

Carry on.

AFTERWORD

by Kabir Sehgal

In times of darkness, we must return to the light. When there is fear, let us remember to hope. And when there is evil, let's not lose faith that goodness will emerge.

We're living through incredibly tumultuous times. The year 2020 may be known in the history books just by its number, like 1776 or 1865, 1918 or 1945. The world has suffered immensely as the COVID-19 pandemic has taken the lives of hundreds of thousands. The United States has been acutely affected by the virus, and as of this writing in the fall of 2020, there seems to be no end in sight. Millions of Americans are sequestered in their homes, trying to avoid getting infected. The public health crisis has metastasized into a jobs crisis and economic recession that will have lasting consequences on how we work.

At the same time, systemic racial injustice in the United States has been brought to the fore yet again with the police killings of Michael Brown, George Floyd, Breonna Taylor, and countless other victims of unspeakable, racially charged violence. These disgraceful acts have led to a public and sustained outcry for justice, equality, and reform. Since the Trayvon Martin murder, the Black Lives Matter movement has awakened millions to the importance of identifying and eliminating racial biases in individuals and institutions.

The United States is beleaguered with a spate of challenges. We're sick, tired, and angry. And there is tremendous sadness.

We must chart a path to a brighter, more peaceful future. With America enduring such an arduous period, now is the time to return to one of the sagest voices among us—someone who had been steady and steadfast in his convictions and who had the moral authority to guide us to higher ground.

Congressman John Lewis went through the crucible of racial conflict and violence. As the chairman of the Student Nonviolent Coordinating Committee (SNCC), he served on the front lines of the civil rights movement with Dr. Martin Luther King Jr. in the 1960s. He helped to alchemize the energy of the movement into the permanence of law, enshrined in the Civil Rights Act of 1964 and the Voting Rights Act of 1965. He was the last remaining individual of the "big six" leaders of the civil rights movement. As a member of Congress for thirty-three years, he helped give a voice to the voiceless and advocate for civil and human rights for all. He was not just the conscience of the Congress but reflected the generous spirit and resilient character of our country.

America needs John Lewis.

When Gretchen Young shared with me her vision for this project, I immediately jumped aboard. I couldn't imagine not being part of something that honors his life and legacy. In fact, years ago, I was with the congressman in his Washington, DC, office when Gretchen presented her idea for what would become his book *Across That Bridge*.

I am honored to have known several civil rights leaders, including Ambassador Andrew Young, and I am blessed to have him as my godfather. John Lewis was a family friend since the late 1980s, when he came to my father's office to discuss local business and political matters. Growing up in Atlanta, I have seen firsthand the good and heroic works of the congressman. I was lucky to have spent time with him and to have spoken with him countless times over the decades, and I continue to learn from his example.

He had such a generous, giving spirit. He spent time with my family during the Centennial Olympic Games in 1996. He spoke (and sang) at my mother's nonprofit organization's event that benefitted at-risk children. He took part in my forthcoming musical project that highlights civil rights, delivering a speech with passion and verve. And then there was the time that I joined him and a small delegation on his annual pilgrimage to Selma, where we marched across the Edmund Pettus Bridge and he recounted what happened on Bloody Sunday. This memory still gives me chills, a pinch-me, all-time life moment. When I got back on the bus with the group, he sat next to me as we drove back to Birmingham. We spoke on a range of topics from infrastructure projects in Alabama to the best places in Atlanta to eat Southern cooking.

It was indeed solemn speaking to Congressman Lewis during his last months. Though I knew his health was declining quickly, I was still devastated upon learning of his passing. But I slowly started to see how this book project could take on new meaning—connecting the dots between the civil rights leader of yesteryear and those on the front lines today.

It has been a privilege to help bring this book into the world. And it wouldn't have happened without the indefatigable Michael Collins, the embodiment of grit and grace, who served Lewis as his chief of staff. I am inspired with how Michael navigated the last few months of the congressman's life, from handling always demanding congressional duties to making sure Lewis was receiving the best care.

Throughout this book Lewis is hopeful and optimistic about the future of our country. Despite being diagnosed with pancreatic cancer, he was resolute: "I have a fighting chance." That this legendary and towering American civil and human rights leader faced his own personal health struggle with determination revealed his courage and grace. In this time of darkness, he was not deterred or dismayed. He kept hope alive and was unflappable in his faith.

I like to think that Congressman Lewis was smiling from heaven during the 2020 elections.

Not only did Georgia turn blue—a manifestation of years of hard work and organizing by grassroots activists—but his pastor, Reverend Raphael Warnock, and his intern, Jon Ossoff, were both elected U.S. senators, which changed the control of the Senate—and the direction of our country. This new leadership has the power to enact measures that will create positive change in the lives of millions of Americans. Our leaders can and must implement policies—like fairer voting rights—for which Congressman Lewis fought.

We hope that John Lewis's *Carry On: Reflections for a New Generation* will provide a meaningful meditation and spiritual statement on where we are in our journey to "redeem the soul of America," as he puts it. His comments will surely help all of us reflect upon what we should do as individuals and citizens. By heeding his example and living by his values, we can remain resilient and grow together as we face the challenges ahead.

JOHN LEWIS CHRONOLOGY

1940   Lewis is born near Troy, Alabama, to share-cropper parents.

1951   On a visit to relatives in Buffalo, New York, Lewis experiences a desegregated society for the first time.

1958   Lewis meets Dr. Martin Luther King Jr. for the first time. Years later, Lewis will say that King taught him "to be optimistic, to never get lost in despair, to never become bitter, and to never hate."

1959   As a college student in Nashville, Lewis

learns the principles of nonviolent protest while attending a series of workshops conducted by the Reverend James Lawson. The workshops evolve into the Nashville Student Movement (NSM), which begins staging sit-ins at area lunch counters to protest racial inequality.

1961   Lewis is assaulted repeatedly (most notably in Rock Hill, South Carolina; Birmingham; and Montgomery) as one of the original Freedom Riders—young Black and white people who used the interstate buses to protest segregation in the South. Lewis will be arrested—some two dozen times by 1963—for his role in the ongoing protests.

1963   Lewis becomes chairman of the Student Nonviolent Coordinating Committee (SNCC), an organization dedicated to direct-action protests against segregation and Black disenfranchisement.

1963   Lewis helps organize and lead the March

on Washington as the youngest member of the iconic "big six," a group that included King, A. Philip Randolph, James Farmer, Whitney Young, and Roy Wilkins. King delivers his "I Have a Dream" speech, but Lewis is persuaded to tone down his own remarks criticizing the Kennedy administration's commitment to civil rights.

1965   Lewis and Hosea Williams, King's chief lieutenant in the Southern Christian Leadership Conference (SCLC), lead 600 activists out of Selma, Alabama, on a march to the state capital in Montgomery to protest the disenfranchisement of Black voters in the South. The protesters are attacked by baton-wielding police while attempting to cross the Edmund Pettus Bridge; 17 demonstrators are hospitalized, and Lewis suffers a fractured skull. Televised images of "Bloody Sunday" stun the nation and spur President Johnson to submit a voting rights bill to Congress.

1968   Lewis marries Lillian Miles. The couple will have one child together, John-Miles Lewis.

1970   Lewis becomes director of the Voter Education Project, which adds nearly 4 million minority citizens to the voting rolls during the seven years of his leadership.

1981   Lewis is elected to the Atlanta City Council.

1986   Lewis is elected to the U.S. House of Representatives from Georgia's 5th District. He will be reelected 16 times, serving, in the words of the *Atlanta Journal-Constitution*, as "the conscience of Congress."

1988   Lewis introduces a bill to create a national African American museum, but Senate Republicans block the measure for 15 successive years. The bill finally passes in 2003, and the National Museum of African American History and Culture officially opens in 2016.

2008   Lewis endorses Barack Obama for president. When asked whether Obama's election represents the fulfillment of Dr. King's dream, Lewis replies, "No, it's just a down payment.... There are still too many people that are being left out and left behind."

2013 Lewis becomes the first U.S. congressman to write a graphic novel. *March: Book One* is the first in a trilogy about the civil rights movement.

2013 Lewis is one of 8 Democratic lawmakers arrested after staging a sit-in in front of the Capitol to call for immigration reform. It is his 45th arrest, and his third as a member of Congress, for getting into "good trouble."

2016 Saying "We have been too quiet for too long," Lewis leads a sit-in on the House floor to protest a refusal by Republicans to allow a vote on gun control.

2020 Lewis endorses Joe Biden for president and publicly recommends that he select a woman of color as his running mate.

2020   Lewis passes away, after a battle with pancreatic cancer. Former president Barack Obama delivers the eulogy, saying: "He, as much as anyone in our history, brought this country a little bit closer to its highest ideals."

ABOUT THE AUTHOR

Congressman John Lewis (1940–2020) was a leader in the American civil rights movement. He was chairman of the Student Nonviolent Coordinating Committee (SNCC), played a key role in the struggle to end segregation, and was an avid proponent of voting rights—including fighting for the John R. Lewis Voting Rights Act of 2020, renamed after him in memoriam. Despite more than forty arrests, physical attacks, and serious injuries, John Lewis remained a devoted advocate of the philosophy of nonviolence. The author of *Walking with the Wind: A Memoir of the*

Movement, an autobiography of his activism, John Lewis was the recipient of numerous awards from national and international institutions, including the Lincoln Medal, the John F. Kennedy "Profile in Courage" Lifetime Achievement Award (one of only two ever bestowed), and the NAACP Spingarn Medal.